FOLLOW THE LIGHT

AMY DUVALL-MEHRINGER

FOLLOW THE LIGHT. Copyright © 2023 Inspirtainment Unlimited. All rights reserved.

Photographs by Amy Duvall-Mehringer.

Artwork by M. Brandon Rosbrook.

Cover and formatting by RKS Hobbs.

ISBN: 9798863715056

10 9 8 7 6 5 4 3 2 1

FOR SUNNY

WHO GAVE ME THE COURAGE TO
SHARE MY VOICE

FOREWORD

> "In the middle of the journey of our life,
> I came to myself within a dark wood
> where the straight way was lost.
> Ah, how hard a thing it is to tell what a wild,
> and rough, and stubborn wood this was,
> which in my thought renews my fear!"
> -Dante Alighieri, The Divine Comedy

In 2012, I committed to writing a poem a day. Three days after I made this commitment, I woke up in what has been called by others the "dark night of the soul". Prior to this, I never would have written about my suffering, but since I already made the commitment I decided to follow through with it.

Flash forward a year later, and I had written just over a thousand poems. Not all were great, but it felt like a great achievement, nonetheless, I continued to write poetry for the next few years, though not as prolifically as that first year. With hard work and faith, I worked toward my dreams once again.

Then, in 2018, just when it seemed that all of my effort was beginning to come to fruition, *everything stopped.* I found myself not in a dark wood, but outside of the world, completely, trapped in a void of vast emptiness. That is the place from which I wrote the first poem in this book, "Maybe This".

In the days, months, years after I became empty, I learned to let go of what I had thought was my life's purpose. I grieved and accepted all that I had lost, suffered through, dedicated myself toward, prayed for, ached and stayed alive for. I found myself accepting life on its terms, as it came to me, finding joy in moments instead of expecting it constantly.

One evening in 2021, I looked out the window at the sun setting through the trees while I washed the dinner dishes, and it came to me. It was time that I realized my dreams. I was going to record the album I had always wanted to make, and I was going to publish books of poetry.

And now as I write this in October 2023, both of these things are at last happening. My first album, *Love Letters on the Path,* has just been released, and *Follow the Light* is my first book of poems.

I hope the words that I felt inspired to say can help you on your journey. I feel that by reading this book, you and I have connected in a way that makes us friends. As my friend, I wish for you to have courage and hope on your own journey, to learn to speak to and for yourself in new, honest ways, and that you open yourself to all of the possibilities of this wonderful, terrible, beautiful world we live in.

As we follow the light,

Amy xoxo

FOLLOW THE LIGHT

Maybe This

We wandering stars
    be always coming home to ourselves
When wandering far
    be ever present to the truth:
        No one is coming to save you
        Because you don't need saving
You just need to round the next corner of the road
    after sitting on a few friends' benches
    to rest your weary, wandering bones

This could be the place to finish you off
    making way for a new beginning of you
    to become everything you never knew you could be
All your dreams could die here—
        mutilated on a dirty gym floor—
        burned up by the anger of others
        and the trauma you shed like your shoes
        before that holy, dancing flame
    Abrupt, pain-filled losses
        leading you into the still, empty spaces
        within a deep, wordless death

    Maybe you will never utter another written word
    Maybe you are not ever meant
        to do anything more for the world at large
        than what you have already done
    Maybe it will be enough to simply live from here
        without a larger dream
        of changing anyone or anything

    Maybe all you need to do to change everything
        is to sing the songs
        coming from your soul's aching
        and then lay down and rest awhile
        beside the one who loves you

Red Sun Rising

Red sun
    rising above on-ramps
Orange and gold orbs dancing on silver water
        love bridged
            abridged
                unabridged
            prayer ascending and descending
        ethereal mist surrounds baseline
            treetops
                towers
                    cranes
                        bridges
Floating up from this magical smokiness
    this morning's color therapy
        red
            orange
                brown
                    white
                gold
            bronze
        copper

Fall sits in blazing splendor
    this December beginning
        revealed spots of hidden beauty
           all along commutes
                portals into mystery
            at every bending moment
        of God-paths
    every where
Work waits to steal the beauty of my wanderlust
            but for now...
I smile
    at the courage of all these leaves letting go
        simply jumping with abandon
            without nets
                free falling into their next adventures
        at the extreme holy beauty of this very moment
I carry this with me
    changing the landscape of my day
        holding this sacred space
            returning again and again
                to dip my feet into the colors
                    of my mindful remembering

Sunny Days and Ashes

The years
    walking for miles
    stop
    stand still
    free
    easy
I live in a sunny
    smudgy
    day of ashes
Scattered all around the world
On open fields of foreheads
Walking billboards of humility
Dusty towns and streets
Where harp strings
    release dreams
    long longed for
Cascading rainbows twirl in the wind

Candy Floss,
    the tree outside my window,
    dances in pre-spring air
She plays with her hair
Smiling she whispers,
"Relax, my sweet,
We're all just angels fallen from grace."

Faces Within the Sacred Mist

I see your faces within the sacred mist
women of the seven mountains
emerging through your veiled masks
your lovely smiling photographs
white clouds descended into tree tops
forest of beauty hung with shadow
ghostly opaque beauty
black fury assembled
the voice of heaven demanding silence
our stories tumble into this place
honest and life-changing
I am listening
I am letting go of all illusory beliefs
that you and I are not enough
this magic moment holds us fully
light breaking through in patches of holy wonder
all these doors into unlimited possibility
the darkness holds all these shades
and shapes of mystery
I drive a thousand miles
feeling the magnitude of what these days are
where we will all go from here
is a matter of personal choosing
all I know is the world will never be the same for me
because you invited me into your circle
because you held me with so much love and grace
as I worked through the startling reality
of my unexpected resurrection

The Sandpiper Prayer

There are wild prayers stirring inside me
I wonder
    If I was a Sandpiper, what would I pray for?
For the tide to cover my feet in lacy splendor,
Leaving behind breakfast
And that feeling of being purely alive
       in this new morning,
Ready to take off into the wind
       and the large blue sky?
  Yes!
That is also the prayer
          inside myself
Waiting to be spoken
The wild prayer of wonder and gratitude
      and of gathering myself
               for flight

Valley Songs

Moving slowly
With ease and grace
New moon hiding briefly
Before moving on into the new circle
Of waxing and waning
Fullness and funness at the center of its continuous circling

This oracle of contemporary and ancient sacredness

Flowing free
Into the Crystal River
Running through threads
Of purest gold
Where fire and glass meet
I will touch your soul
And dance with you forever

I WILL TOUCH YOUR SOUL
AND DANCE WITH YOU FOREVER

Dance

Show up as the lover of your own life
Kiss me in the shadow of that new moon
Ready to break into the future with full shine
Hold me beneath the milky glow of your fullest glowing
Take hold of the silver threads
        unraveling their mystery in the deep night sky
Remember within yourself: intensity evokes magic
Celebrate your Unbirthday with a party involving sweetness
As you step into this brand new day -
        this new version of yourself
Deep is always calling to deep
Circles are always circling within circles
Sacred spirals, leading you on
Gentle rain, watering your growth
Stand under the waterfalls of wonder and curiosity
Let grace flow over your head
Speak with courage the words rising
        within your luscious mouth
Sing with the beautiful voice hidden within your soul
Then take off your shoes and dance

Do You Want to go to Heaven?

Tables are turning
Prophecies are coming true
Predictions from old
     standing stark naked
        in front of the cheering crowd
Scotland's burning
Smoke begins to rise
Mirrors reflect our need to be right
In spite of the consequences
Can we simply let the moment slip by unchallenged
Melting gracefully into a new morning
Where we will not go to war anymore?
Young men growing old from living peacefully
Laughter and love all they will ever know

Everybody talks about heaven
But nobody really wants to go there

Lullaby

Listen to another channel
Not the same old one
      you've been listening to all your life
Not your mama's critique
Or your daddy's yelling that you are not enough
Give away your sister's old clothes
And your brother's painful sarcasm
Open up a pretty bottle and celebrate
Speak into a deeper purpose for life right now
Openly share your fears and your heart's longings
Eat, laugh together
Go deep
Go light
Listen to everything
Sing songs
Hug tight
Sleep sweet

Prisoner

There is no escape from the higher themes of my life
Moving into
As above so below
Mirror, mirror
Hearts burning alive

The problem of this sector is like smoke sitting in my lungs
Crazy dreams help me let go of the old traumas

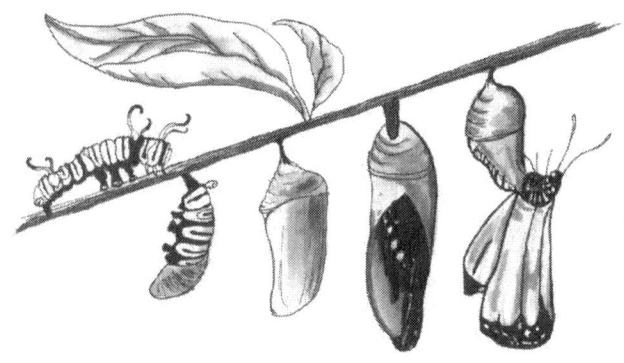

As the butterfly emerges
Evolves
Becomes
Beauty captivates
I will be its prisoner
Feed me forever
until I die

Freedom

Let me let go into the wild free song of the nightingale
Let me dance the wild free dance of the grouse
Let me embrace my voice in public with grace
Let me shout of the joy you have given me
Let me speak tender words of love
Let me sing with abandon as a robin in spring
Let me fly as the ducks in skeined formation,
      perfection in the fall air
Let me forget,
      as the ones who have lost their memory
      forget their social learning
Release my fear
Free my life
Free my song

You Belong

Shock and awe
Fill this night sky
Ushering in the dark
Welcoming the spirit
Get yourself grounded
Before you bow on holy ground
Laugh and be easy in these moments of grace
You are welcome here
You belong in this reverent place
Stand in the sunshine of love
Surrender everything
      as murky waters run crystal
Listen deeply to the music of your life's song

Once in a Blue Moon

Once in a blue moon
        comes a year of miracles
Beyond the answers
        to the beautiful questions
            waiting in the fields of past years
            or the winding paths of the future

Once in a blue moon
        there is a full moment of rapture
Born to be wild
        Means the same thing
        Yet this moment is unique
        In every single
        Solitary
        Life

For Miles

From this bench
I can see for Miles
Miles
        and
                Miles
                      and
                            Miles
                                  and Miles to come-
Each mile has informed my living
        has had vast impact
        in my heart
Letting go is my continual lifework
        surrender my career
I've let go of everyone,
        everything,
I've ever loved.
I carry them,
        green, rooted trees,
        within me.

I am done with questions,
        even the beautiful ones.

I am committed to this process of my becoming.

I am a force of the nature of love.

I have no regrets, no demands.

I fly with the seagulls,
        bend low before the burning bushes;
I sit in the holy hush of the sound of silence,
        letting go,
                letting go,
        seeking new understanding.
The deep places within me
        give thanks for each piece of love,
        for each of these miles
                I have experienced.
The blue sky shouts out to me
        all that is coming:
                the best is always yet to be.
Coming to me and through me
        as I break through the newly discovered
                hardened edges of my heart
                      to allow
                              freedom
                                    for you
                                          and
                                              for me

THE JOURNEY

I AM DONE WITH QUESTIONS
EVEN THE BEAUTIFUL ONES

The Journey

The journey of a thousand miles
    Finds the road-weary warrior
        Avoiding that first step as long as possible

Prayer is not for the wise
    But for the needy and fragile

Understanding hearts get so tired of breaking

Jesus came for the heartbroken
The tired souls saddled up
    regardless of personal cost
Those who would pass through the needles' eye
    despite the obvious challenges
    of that calling
        facing confrontations of Biblical proportions
Red Sea overflowing its banks
    with hell dogs and wild chariots at their heels
Only at the final resolve of toes forward
    sucked into surging waves
    will they ever find
    that becoming dry ground
Oh the mystery of second sight

Battle-tested faith is not a wise endeavor
    for this is the vision only prayer can bring
    brilliant light of the soul's-eye
    around the bend of practical living
Right there birthed into the physical
    from the spiritual realm
    beginning seeds of our Annual Festivals of Glory
Each started with fear and trembling
    words of vulnerability
    turning victorious
    as we make way for the miracle
    to work through us
    in spite of us

Trumpets and rams horns blowing at sundown
    as we humbly say the words
    of grace
    of truth
    of thanks:
        Thus far LOVE has brought us
            Only LOVE can mend a heart
            Change the world
                Bring us home

THE JOURNEY

The Way You Love Me

Apples of silver
Roses of blue
The way you love me
The way I love you

Raspberry mornings
Blueberry nights
The way you love me
Fills up my life

Baby-blue kisses
Fingertips touch
The way you love me
Within the hush

PJs for dinner
Naked for bed
The way you love me
Goes to my head

Neon cowboys
Pale shades of white
The way you love me
All through the night

Mountain of stars
Yellowstone trees
The way you love me
So wild and so free

Music-filled mornings
Music-filled nights
The way you love me
Always feels right

Poems and posies
Cookies and tea
The way you love me
Just let it be

The Rocks Are Wise

The rocks are wise and kind
      holding blood and bone
      close to their souls
Dust from past death
      love and anger
They carry colors of sunshine and rain
      containers of joy and sorrow
      radiating love
      cheering us on
They hold gushing water
      ready for our thirst in a faith-filled strike
      or a word spoken in times of obedience
Vibrating at such a high soul-level
      songs of celebration and canticles of morning
      songs of broken heartedness and grief and mourning
They are ready to hold me steady
      to burst into song to match my mood
      when I am silent to make me laugh
      to chill my butt when I am cold
      to warm my heart when I am lonely
      to listen with care when I am silent
They sit in company

They create my borders
        and speak great and wondrous volumes
        of my beauty and value
        and with that,
        I arrive back at my first thought...

The rocks are wise and kind
        Foundational friends
        True-blue partners
                Providing harmony and balance
                In every word they choose,
                      ever so intentionally,
                          to say

THE ROCKS ARE WISE

IN THE GARDEN

In the blink of a proverbial eye
    there I went
    taking an evolutionary
    leap of faith forward
        fast
    not knowing whithersoever I went-
Yet, here I stand,
    having Landed in this Edenic Garden.

I have to laugh at God,
    just gratuitously showing off,
    with more beauty than my heart can hold,
    yet still holding firm to the same old lines,
      "Please stay on the path"
      "Look for snakes"
    and other such helpful signs
      (Ironic eyeroll here)

He, posting the rules to The Garden this time,
having gained some wisdom from our last experience here.

He, knowing me so well,
from walking the pilgrimage together these past thirty years.

Yes, I am prone to wander.
I feel it most of the time...

Angels hover near as I walk back home,
        finding black feathers tipped in white.
It's an Amazing day to remember.

Poetry is such a beautiful snapshot.
I will write about these special days,
        of getting to know Billy Collins so very personally.
My wine and empty plate,
        which held my lobster dip and Triscuits,
        sitting in companionable silence
        as we listened to your day way back then,
        and I blew bubbles into the waiting arms
        of a blooming tree
                (whose name is Candy Floss)
        beside my tiny petal-strewn deck
on a perfect day
in Rock Hill, South Carolina

Spirit Moving Wild

Spirit moving wild
      in early morning watches
Hard-time trees dancing furiously
      to the drumbeat of stormy weather
      In the strobed silver lightning of pre-dawn 5am
The air is thick like wet velvet
      breath of God is palpable
      on my cool skin
Hot creamy coffee, my morning lover
      entering my body with tender eagerness
The sun-catcher has become a moon-catcher
      creating stars in this moment of chaos
      twinkling merrily to my right
The flowers laugh with the excitement of the moment

I sit still within this electric energy
      alive with sensuous delight
      bare feet to the ground
      the aroma of all this grand, holy beauty filling me
It is the morning after the resurrection
      and all heaven and nature are still celebrating
      in glamorous style

IT IS THE MORNING AFTER THE
RESURRECTION
AND ALL OF HEAVEN AND EARTH
ARE CELEBRATING

MORNING GRACE

This morning the sun hides
    behind gray, opaque skies
        resting a while from the glorious spotlight
The trees speak louder than normal
    and the blood-red of the geranium
        shouts like an energetic motivational speaker
The whole western world,
    or at least my small patch of the woods,
    is covered in the green-gray dust
    left from the orgy of the trees and the bees
    not holding back their enthusiasm,
        beauty, or excitement.
Wild lovers
    dancing furiously
    in the erotic winds
    of spring.
The world is alive
    right outside my open window
    cool wind seeping through
    the slightly rusted screen
    to enlarge my morning heart
The birds sing their own songs
    at the same time
    not minding at all
    that they are each singing their own
Somehow it all makes perfect sense
    and I leave the grand questions of the ages
    and the conspiracy theories of eager revolutionists
    on the table for others to wrestle
    as I bow in sheer astonishment
        of the wonder that I am alive
        and whisper a simple
            "Thank you"

THE SECRET TO LIFE

In the middle of the newest pandemic
      every bite of food feels like luxury
      to those of us not living in fear
Just savoring every beautiful bite of gratitude
      keeping us strong and healthy

Those of us not stockpiling for the end of the world
Those of us practicing distance
      in care of those who are weaker
Those of us trusting 'today's bread' is enough bread
Trusting today's toilet paper
      will be enough to get us through
          the roughest of these gut-stressing moments
Trusting whatever we need more of
      will come to us in perfect time
Miracles are happening everywhere
      just like they normally are
Maybe we're finally moving slowly enough
      to notice a few more of them

      That would be a nice thing, wouldn't it?

      Maybe that's enough

In a world where we take so much for granted
      and seem surprised at our vulnerability
Maybe enjoying the simple pleasures of this moment-
      This bite of sublime key lime pie
          is the real secret to a wonderful life

Three Sundays

Right in the middle of three Sundays in April ,
    make that glorious decision
        to put down what is not yours to carry.
Remember, wise one,
        if it doesn't make your heart sing,
        it is not yours.
Abandon it right here
        in the messy, muddy, middle ground .
Don't give it a second thought.
Just walk away, clean slate,
        up the beautifully curving staircase
        into the wide and waiting arms
        of the friendly field of clover.

Ready to find your true voice in the world?
Write the truest poems you can find inside you,
        the words plucked from your eager senses
        who've been waiting for a lifetime
        to tell you what they love so deeply.
Then speak those magical words
        of your own true happiness
        to the four corners of the joyous earth.
After you have walked,
        written
            and spoken,
                sit in silence for days,
                or decades, if necessary-
                  there is no hurry.
                Your life is here to savor.
Slow down to the speed of poetry;
        sway to the time of jazz.
Take it a line at a time.
Follow it deeper and deeper
        until you hear the voice
        you know is your own.

Everything Stopped

The way everything stopped
in deafening silence
after that flash of yellow,
after the soft, yet solid thud
that I heard reverberated inside me
like a bell
after that terrible flash.

The way the heated, afternoon sun
still kept on flashing its rainbows
in crazy various directions
at the whim of the spring breeze;
the way my heart,
pounding loud,
pulled me towards the open doorway
with anxious hope and prayerful dread;
the way life caught in my throat;
The way warm relief waved over my body,
bottom-to-top
then top-to-bottom,
as I saw your tiny body, lying upside-down,
golden feathers softly moving
in time with your still-beating, beautiful heart;
the way I watched, still and silent,
holding you close inside,
having felt the same way on multiple occasions
when life dealt me a sudden knockout blow
when I was flying along full-speed.

Then, as I waited with you, breathing quietly,
you moved your splayed-out feathers,
turned over onto your small feet,
resting quietly as long as you needed
with no fear or hurry,
recovering from the shock of hitting that
unseen, unexpected, clear glass.

You and I connected
in this eternal moment
in so many ways
as you visited my nest
for a little minute-
and then, with a soft hop
and a full body shake,
you lifted off
and flew away,
sure and steady,
without looking back,
leaving me with the feeling
you had taught me what I needed to know,
and someday soon
I could possibly follow you
into the evening sky.

EVERYTHING STOPPED

Someday soon
I will follow you
into the evening sky

I Was Taught

I was taught to stand in line
I was taught it's not my time
I was taught to people-please
I was taught to bend my knees
I was taught to raise my hand
I was taught I need a man
I was taught to never speak
I was taught to *not* move my feet
I was taught that I was wrong
I was taught I don't belong
I was taught my church was right
I was taught a certain fight
I was taught I wouldn't finish
I was taught I should diminish
I was taught to take abuse
I was taught to just excuse
I was taught to obey
I was taught to walk away
I was taught that I was vain
I was taught to live in pain
I was taught to live in fear
I was taught to not drink beer
I was taught the way to heaven
I was taught on May eleven
I was taught I didn't matter
I was taught that hearts will shatter
I was taught to give and give
I was taught these rules to live
I was taught I must say "yes"
I was taught I was a mess
I was taught to stay and die
I was taught to live a lie
I was taught that love meant loss
I was taught money is boss
I was taught to say "I'm fine"
I was taught that words should rhyme

Then I turned and found the way
To learn a new thing everyday

To break the chains

To teach myself

To love my life

To grow and heal

To love and know

To just be real

To share my words

To break those rules

To speak my truth

To say my "no's"

To dance my dance

To sing my song

To go my way

To be set free

To live my heart

To just be me

...THEN I LEARNED

The Shift

My heart is feeling the pull of the faithful tides,
moon falling in love with the ebb and flow of me,
wind on the waves ruffling feathered white waters,
ocean-blue with no end in sight.
Sand getting all up in my personal business,
feeling infinitesimal now in this grand horizon
of the eternal perspective.

My melancholy moments shift into moments
of unutterable holiness,
with the gulls riding the gusts in complete trust.

Mind melting into peaceful surrender,
standing with the great blue heron
waiting for the signal to fly,
with this visioned glimpse of my own piece
in the grand wholeness.

The world is mine.
Patience: my most valuable virtue,
even as I acknowledge
I have no control over anything,
especially my next breath
or my next meal.

My feet have found their way
into the green, green grass of everything
on my journey homeward,
into my deepest mystery.

Feeling the memory of your touch
with the wild blue waves
as they call
and call
and call…

Rising

Rising with the morning wind
On a wing and a prayer
Moving ever higher
Floating on thin air

Shifting my perspective
From this view on higher ground
Beauty now surrounds me
I feel angels all around

Above the storm
I'm free, I fly
I will live
Before I die

And I'm rising up to meet you
On a wing and a prayer

Take Off Your Shield of Lies
(A Talk to Myself)

Take off your shield of lies and stop cheating yourself on what you most deserve.

Bring your deepest longings into the light.

Start living your own way.

Start speaking your own truth.

Let go of the bullshit story that commitment doesn't matter and that you can continue to live secretly instead of breaking your old, worn-out vows.

Get proud of yourself, girl, for doing hard things- for letting your comfort slide in favor of a juicy life.

Begin learning and knowing in new ways.

Remember to bow and humbly become foolish in the vision of your own self.

Know that your version of the deep end of the pool is someone else's kiddie pool; stop thinking the fish painted on the bottom is the ocean floor.

Just stop thinking so damn much so you can live your passion. Come up for air before you drown in four inches of water.

Breathe deep gulps of gratitude, then shout the truest sentence you've ever spoken and walk on into your biggest adventure.

Morning Comes

Morning comes
strong as an ox
hotter than hell
until thunder
sleeping behind a curtain of clouds
awakens like a grumpy giant
throwing his weight around

Yods
Yins
&
Yangs
moving fast
in this stifling heat
making no great wind
just a faint, gentle breeze
to cool the purple and pink dancing blooms

Life slowly moving into balanced places
lightening loads by sudden revelation
joy winding its way up the path
into its hearted home
love finds its ground in the blending of souls

Hold the feather
in your open palm
&
blow

MYSTERIES

There are mysteries in the air today.

We are seeking to walk into the sunshine,
    feel fresh air blowing in our faces
    against the wind.

Sing me a new love song.

Revelation can be intimidating,
Nothing less than ruthless,
Until you raise your vibration to meet it head on.

Get ready for a ride with a wild hare;
Get in some self-care and
    take your vitamins
    then hold on to your hat-

Good things are coming
    regardless of the circumstance.

The plan is bigger than you can see:

    Zoom out
    Zoom out
    Zoom out

Some Days

Some days words aren't easy
It's like a blank grey wall of cloud
sitting inside
not wanting to reveal any lurking idea
which might be living or dying behind it

In one way
it's an easy, empty way to be in the morning
in another
it's a bit disconcerting
to find no words rattling around
inside of myself
no beauty waiting to be put into words
spilled out onto white paper
nothing to show
nothing to prove
my existence for this day

Is this how non-poets feel?
People who never draw ink out
like their own blood
to dry or run with tears

Mixed media of expression
The history of my longing
The burning man of my desires
flaming into life itself
The sun waiting to rise
until I have a way to record its colors
in some exquisitely lettered way
only I can say

YAHWEH

mother earth
father sky
mother birth
father time
peace will never come through power
peace will only come when there is *humility*
no desire for power

the circles of polarity are balanced
kindness is not weakness
weakness is not kindness
love is not enabling
enabling is not love
self-care is not selfishness
and selfishness is not self-care

we cannot exist without each other
say it again:
female and male cannot exist without each other
equal: not interchangeable!
all souls *equal*

one true GOD
both mother and father
creator of all
breath of the world
light and life
YAHWEH

love
equal
peace
equal
male
equal
female
equal
we are one
equal
connected
when one suffers we all suffer

lead us
deliver us from power
deliver us from ourselves
allow us to glimpse with new sight
humble us to receive
reveal YOURSELF
forgive our arrogance
our lack of gratitude
our desire for power
YAHWEH
even now
bring us peace

The Dreaming Tree

the night takes me into its absorbing darkness
    wrapping me in its enveloping cashmere arms
tomorrow's tales remain unrevealed
    time out of time in this moment of now

I tried to grab the fog… I mist

the dreaming tree singing Don Williams' songs
    carries me deep into my waiting heart

my drum beats out of time with the world at large
    with holy wonder
    and beautiful solitude
    yet beautifully connected
    to the whole shebang
shenanigans playing wild and free with a soul
    holding space for beautiful sorrow
    at the water's edge
I fly into the dark night
    scattered
    smothered
    and covered
fortune tells our tale of greatest luck
    as only lovers can
wisest fortunes thrown in
    together at the right moment
    deeply breathing
finest life and dearest death
    equally beneficial to the big picture
I choose the left-hand side of everything you offer
headlight beams pointing to the future
    in the gathered darkness
I hear your voice in my ear
    as the wind's caress takes me home

THE DREAMING TREE

A Little

a little prayer
a little light
a little moon
a little night

a little solemn
a little silly
a little rest
a little busy

a little smoke
a little mirror
a little thinking
a little clearer

a little major
a little minor
a little feather
a little finer

a little hum
a little throttle
a little ship
a little bottle

a little grace
a little charity
a little faith
a little clarity

Strike the Sun

Strike the sun
Speak to the moon
Stand between the rock and the hard place
    until the mountains crack
    and clear waters flow
Stand firm until you hear the rocks singing
    the songs they have sung
    since the beginning of everything
The orchestra of the mountain
    plays full out
    as the sunset cinema
    completes its brilliant showing
        the last crescendo
        fading into shadowy resolve
        in the gathered darkness
Curtains of silence falling heavy
    as reverie descends
        revealing fixed patterns
        of thought needing
        to surrender and break
            like the mountain itself
Learning springs
    afresh from deep
    calling to deep
    moving unhurried
        gracefully changing landscapes
        hidden from the hawk's great eye
Sky filled with glowing pathways
    towards dreams and higher purpose
        release the miracle of not knowing
Rest easy in the unlimited possibility
    of the possibility of all there is to see

Allow Justice and Mercy
>   into the same bed
>>   those great Lovers of life and joy
Be angry
>   without making a mistake
>>   without losing control
Ok, burn down the house-
>   Just not the people inside
Walk with me
>   towards home
>   where there is
>   always a light on
>   in the window
>>   a fire burning
>>   to warm our conversation
>   always room for company
>   a kettle always hot
>   ready to share a note
>>   its own particular thrill
>>   of you and me
>>>   the singular beauty
>>>   of 2 dirty cups
>>>   in the sink

Rise Up Singing

The way the left hand holds the drama
    the old abuse clinging
        to the sticky self of yesterday
            desperate to die.

Myriad broken promises
        kaliedoscoping down empty corridors
            creating new shapes
                of white-walled memories.

All those Golden Rings long gone
        stolen
        like the fragile innocence of that woman-child
    taken by evil forces
        wearing velvet over rusted iron
            cloaked in words of loving illusion

Does your thumb
    ache to sing
    all the songs
    you wrote as a child
        before you were afraid
        to dance to your own rhythm?
Will you let the cool air
    flow over unshackled wrists
        as you remember?

It is for freedom
>   *for this exact moment*
>   that you ran the brutal gauntlet
>   burning the bridges
>   as you went over
>   into the promised land.

This is the good morning
>   for you to rise up singing
>   all the birds in flight ready on the wing
>   to assist you in any way you need
>   and heaven's angels waiting eagerly
>   to cheer you on
>   and hear you sing again

Prayer

Prayer is inhale and exhale
Prayer is deepest feeling
Prayer is an action
Prayer is awaiting
Prayer is allowing
Prayer is second sight
Prayer is gratitude
Prayer is complaint
Prayer is touching
Prayer is trusting
Prayer is beyond rational
Prayer is letting go
Prayer is growing larger or smaller
Prayer is bending down or standing tall
Prayer is hands open
Prayer is palms together
Prayer is knees bent
Prayer is head bowed
Prayer is sharing pleasure
Prayer is sharing pain
Prayer is blue sky
Prayer is rain
Prayer is face upturned
Prayer is complete recognition
Prayer is not knowing a thing
Prayer is constant conversation
Prayer is being completely emptied
Prayer is full to the brim

Prayer is moving into the mystery of everything
Prayer is new revelation
Prayer is knowledge older than time
Prayer is selfless death
Prayer is new resurrection
Prayer is letting go of yesterday
Prayer is holding out for the best is yet to come
Prayer is entering the holy silence
Prayer is eyes open
Prayer is eyes closed
Prayer is savoriest tasting
Prayer is wonder and astonishment
Prayer is grit and grime
Prayer is fog and thunderstorm
Prayer is sunshine and shadows
Prayer is complimentary companionship
Prayer is sturdy relationship
Prayer is growing strength
Prayer is evolving intimacy
Prayer is the choir's hallelujah
Prayer is the mother's lullaby
Prayer is patience
Prayer is practice
Prayer is a little bit softer now
    ...a little bit softer now
      ...a little bit softer now

The Other Side

I come out the other side
    of midnight
        or conjunctions of a grand kind
            a bit tired and worn
                but ready for the next step
                on the journey
            the next level of spirit learning
        letting go of everything
      known and unknown
arriving naked into my next morning

I AM

I am learning to be brave.

I am learning to speak my own language.
I am learning who I want to become.
I am learning what kind of life I want to live.
I am learning to stand in my place without flinching.
I am learning to go my own way.
I am learning not to help people who don't want help.
I am learning to embrace my powerful spirit.
I am learning how to build my own bridges,
      complete with lions to guard against the foot-traffic.
I am learning I have value to bring
      to those waiting to hear my voice.
I am learning the intensity of my own burning passions.
I am learning to keep digging
      in the murkiness of my own brokenness.
I am learning to accept my imperfections as beautiful.
I am learning to think in terms of unlimited possibilities.
I am learning I will not always be understood
      in the way I intend.
I am learning to apologize and then move freely forward.
I am learning
      and learning
           and learning
                  new things
                        every minute
                              of every day.
I am learning to be a part of the healing of the world
      because I am learning to be me.

For Such a Time

for such a time as this

what if it all comes down to this moment in time
this arena you stand in right now
this opportunity straight ahead in the path
this pickle
this dilemma
this very hot spot
this moment of crisis

this…

just this…

this choice for you to take it as it is
to rise strong in your glory
to be all that you can be
this very morning

A Small Act

What is a small act of pure love?
Isn't that the ultimate oxymoron?

What matters and what doesn't?
Who decides?

What really rings the captain's bell in the halls of Heaven?
Where are the grandest palaces built?

Who truly owns everything we claim,
everything we hold so dear?

What color will you pick to wear
to the grandest wedding you will ever attend?

When do the people who clean the outhouses
regain their appetites and come to the feast?

Do you believe everyone's poop stinks,
yet is a common element of this thing called "being human"?

Should gratitude protect us from life's hardships?
If I'm thankful, do I get to keep what I want?

Why do some people never know hunger
and others literally starve to death?

Which of the following
is the more important question:

Why me?
Why NOT me?

A Square Moment

a square moment
   a harsh judgement
      a semi-brutal blow
         a hard punch to the gut
           a deadly dance
              an ungodly bigotry
                 an ugly truth stared at
                    a due date gone past
                      a lonely mile
                         a letter unopened
                            a goodbye unsaid
                              an unexpected candidate
                         a gun fight at the ok corral
                    a long expiration
                    a tear for the dearly departed
              a cleansing breath
            a slow turn-around
         an unbearable realization
      a follow-up psalm of surely goodness
   a finishing flourish
a perfect punctuation

an opening trumpet
a brand-new thought
a new inclusion
an age of realism
a decision leaving me high and dry
an imperial compliment of bitter water
a regret left to purge
a thought rolling over and over
an adjustment of consequences
a survival strategy to fall back on
a letting-go to be proud of...
well, sort of...
a flush of birds blown in the wind
a story to forget as soon as possible
a new love to walk into tomorrow
a border of fertile thanksgiving
a few lines drawn in my heart's sand
a few handfuls thrown in my eyes
an opening to learn something new
an opportunity to a new trust
a waterfall to wash it all clean
a nobility to hang my coat on
a path to walk alone

A SQUARE MOMENT

WELCOME HOME

I woke up with thoughts like this:
Never miss an opportunity to give pleasure to someone else.
                          Where is the face I had
                        before the world was made?
Just below the surface of my wearing skin
      is so much joyous future
            waiting to be lived.
I wrote a thought below your name,
    which is tattooed on this heart of mine:
        Greater than happiness is holiness-
                      You could not help me with
                      either of the preceding desires.
Some temples are built without a stone put together;
    God is found where two or three sit
        around a round kitchen table,
           holding hands cupped
                to collect falling tears.
                    How much research will it take
              to release the pain in my shoulders?
Poems and prose are witnesses
    leading to a mapped blueprint of recovery.
                            If I build a house,
        what will the front door look like?
Be still for a long minute,
    then hold the beat one second longer.
                              Welcome home.

Sun on Sunday

I have forgotten how to write a beautiful sentence

I walk through days of dangling participles
jangling questionnaires fall from my lips
black lace Freudian-slips slipping past my fingertips
I adjust my spectacles to see things a new way

Always remember:
poetry comes in multiple formulations
from well-dusted surfaces
to a handmade journal
to carry me safely through another inspired year

To put it bluntly,
I'll take some sun on Sunday, please and thank you
grey skies never looked on so handsomely

Just because I didn't write it down
doesn't mean the poem doesn't exist
Just because I took a new job
doesn't mean I won't sing to you
Just because I didn't call you today
doesn't mean I don't love you
Just because you still make me laugh
doesn't mean I do…

See you on the flip side
I'm too old to die young
but I'll still be beautiful
no matter the weather
I'll still think about you
when the dealin's done

BLUE

I've got all these knotted words
    tangled and broken into pieces
        sitting behind my paint brush
            waiting to flow out
                into the heart of the blue world
Blue is the color of my true love's eyes
    the color of this bruised and hopeful heart of mine
        all the blue notes and blue spaces
            create the music I love most
Blue silence comes to the door of the ocean
    and pulls me out of myself
        into the bluest skies, and the midnight,
            bluer than any other starry night
Angels wear robes of purest blue
    in the presence of my enemies
        who then become my friends
            because blue is the color of friendship
                and blue is the color of my voice
                    speaking truth
When I sing I hope you feel
    blue velvet against your skin
        my lips tracing patterns of love
            into your blood of blue

I come from bluegrass
    and my feet are stained with the sheer delight
        of the colors of my youth
            bare and freckle-faced
                laughing with the yellow sun
                    and blue wind in the high oak trees
I'm always ready to go adventuring
    into the wild blue yonder
        always ready to share
             all our gathered stories
                around the blue flamed fire
Ready to touch the earth
    with bare-naked hands
        and blue suede shoes
Ready to stand, as blue as you, in the falling snow
    ready to play games in blue channels of grace
        ready to turn a new shade of blue
            at a moment's notice
Ready to find out every shade
    of every color
        life has to give
            Hello life
            I'm blue
            How 'bout you?

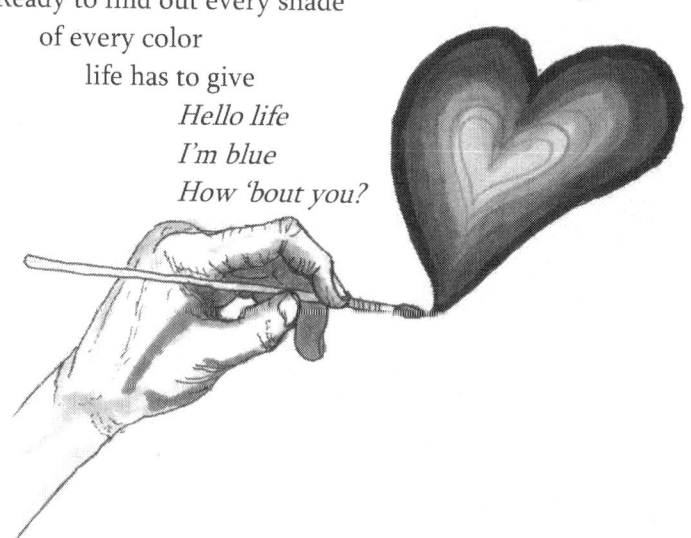

BLUE

Questions of the Day

Which mountain is mine to climb
    out of all the mountains ahead?

Which path, of so many, do I take?
What pieces of me do I leave behind?
What do I take with me for the life ahead?
What rituals make sense in this moment of the journey?
Which voices inspire me and fill me with hope and courage?
What signs are there, just for me,
    in this grand tour of today?
Which conversations are the ones I am called to be a part of?
What delicious foods do I eat with gratitude?
What colors do I hold with delight
    as they warm in my palm?
What heavenly vision do I share?
What hellish remembrance do I withhold?
What can I give away from my abundance?
What is trash?
What is treasure?
What songs do I sing?
Which ones to take out of the playlist?
What ones to never to sing again?
What does it mean to open my heart to another?
What tools do I need to build
    a house of love and belonging?
How do I love someone well?
How do I love someone as they deserve to be loved?
How do I grow my own spirit large and strong,
    and allow others to do the same?

Who will I be at the end of this day?

How can I be even more of myself tomorrow?

THE SADDEST POEM

If I wrote a poem today
it would be the saddest one you would ever read
It would break your heart into small pieces
and scatter them all over the world

It would cause you to cry new oceans into existence,
and all the stars would burn out
from the pain of its essence
global chaos would ensue
the world, as we know it, would end

Therefore, I will not write a poem today
I will wait for another day
when love has found me again
and my heart is a riot of joy
rather than sadness

Then I will write a poem so brilliant
so brimming with happiness
it will create a new heaven
and a new earth
where we will dance forever

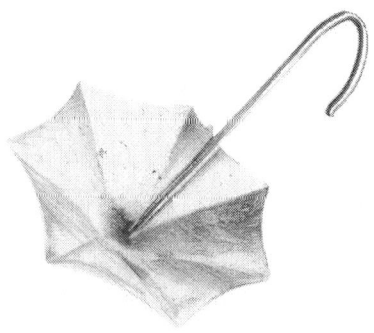

A Few Seconds Before

A few seconds before happiness
    tore poems from my heart
        it occurs to me
            once again
                that everything is grace
Both sides of life's gift are equal
    that to fly free and ride the shining sunbeams
        means trusting your pilot completely
            even in the uneven, scary spaces
                pushing against us
Knowing my pilot opens my soul to sheer beauty
    to rivers of adventure
        cutting through my grids of protection
            through my grasping of thin shreds
                through unnecessary issues of control
I am suddenly aware
    the gates to the kingdom live right here
        opening easily
            when I step forward-
in this confident level of knowing
in this bursting moment of joy
in this perfect snowflake of eternal beauty
    created just to melt unseen by mere mortals
        forever imprinted into this world's history
            just because
                all because
                    in every which way
                because
                of love

Melancholy Prayer

all these colorless rooms
we find ourselves in
the closed doors with locks and chains
the open windows revealing the changing seasons
pictures of our doubt hung fearlessly on white walls
pieces of our lives lined up on mantles
floors marked with tape for the proper place
to stand and perform
or kneel in submission
places to pack and unpack
never quite comfortable enough
to invite company over
dinner for one
is still the loneliest number
the place we come for sleep
sunrooms full of junk
closets ready for upcoming skeletons
life continually tries to get our attention
altars built for gods we continue to ignore
there's more than one way to skin a cat…

but who in hell wants to know even one way???

I think of you sometimes when I find a new bench
it's all I can do
just sit
and think about you
say a melancholy prayer
before stepping forward
into the gathering shadows
of a chilly night

Carry On

cut to the chase, my friend
God dances us
woos us until we can't help falling in love
head over heels

leave the past behind
step into a fresh page
the flow of spirits connecting hearts
to heal our wounds

boil it down to the clearest truth
what does it cost to live our highest life?

distilled wisdom imparted with every word we share
simplicity (distilled beauty),
kindness (distilled love),
authenticity (distilled truth)
are earth's highest spiritual achievements
give me passion for these three gifts of grace

the light always shines out of darkness
stars are not visible in the day skies
candles never stay hidden by a multitude of bushels
the wildfire burns away the dry grasses
a fine sprinkle of salt goes a long way
to the discerning tastebud
laying on of hands warms the whole circle
like a cashmere sweater

we are given choices (free will)
what we choose brings us heaven or hell
don't base your long-term goals on short-term goods
always keep in mind what you want most
think about what you are tolerating once in awhile
look in the mirror to see God's reflection
staple it to your forehead
take it with you
to staple to the foreheads
of everyone you meet

carry on now
carry on

CARRY ON

CANDLES NEVER STAY HIDDEN

Burn

Sometimes it's good to burn things.

Sometimes you need to light the match
of your own life,
then watch the flames grow scarlet
as it consumes the outdated pages
of your soul's words.

The truths you held dear for so long
which no longer ring true,
the vows you must disappoint yourself to break.

Sometimes you must carve a new pattern
in the blood-oath you made so long ago
as an innocent child.

Sometimes you must trust your future self,
the self you don't know yet,
in order to honor your need to change your walking path,
right now in this moment of startling crossroads.

Don't waste another minute.

Light your driest match,
shed your mud-caked shoes
before the flaming pages of your past life.

Give thanks as you let go,
fall to your knees in wonder,
rise as the one who will make a new way
on this blessed earth.

This is holy ground.

Build an altar of all the things
you no longer need to carry.

When you're ready,
take a deep breath
into your new body,
look at the surrounding landscape
with your new eyes,
take out a spotless sheet of paper,
pick up your patient pen,
and write the courageous words
wanting to be born from within you.

BURN

Roses

Roses pouring pink petals
Down and around

Golden strands grounding us to middle earth

If we have a tap root
We can withstand the storms
Feet on solid ground
Trees of green grown rooted and strong

Diamonds on water
Shining

Fierce beauty, the miracle of this world
Heart-aching with so much of everything

This world, the spoken Breath of God
My conversation with love most holy

The only reason for my voice
The highest purpose of my song
The glory of my greatest moments
My joy is always full
        because

You never stopped looking at me
        with that look in your eyes

Age of Aquarius

In this molting Age of Aquarius
with water pouring from aged and busted pipes,
the tin man sits heartlessly rusted in the laundry room,
well beyond any repair.

I see your fragile heart spread out for miles and miles,
love returning from around the bend again and again,
layer after layer of imbedded pain releasing
within each soft, round circle and sharp-edged square.

We are always tenderly held,
pulled from the wreckage of our own spinning brains,
working through nights
of barking dogs and wild hares.

Seasons coming and going,
taking their fine time to bring us out of poverty's grasp,
husks of skin and bone carrying the eerie, ethereal beauty
of life and death within us- our own and all others.

Unmapped blue-skied tomorrows are crossroads
paralleling well-worn pathways on roads less traveled.
Everything is connected by this web of grace-weaving
through our crazy-quilt-patterned ancestral charts.

Our gravestones mark us as brothers and sisters-
we are pushing up daisies as one,
my friend
as well as my foe.

Come to me now,
save me
from destroying myself
in my chosen isolation.

Talk to me in this fine moment
of cabbages and kings;
forgive my sins; save my soul;
take me to the river and wash me clean.

Feed me with roasted chicken,
grapes and sugar plums.
Sing to me the lullabies of my mother
I have loved since childhood

Laugh with me in the face of my worry-stone,
worn smooth by endless hardened time.
Love me like the rock of ages
and never let me go.

AGE OF AQUARIUS

A Love Letter

Thank you, dear heart,

    For being so brave
    For the courage to stay open
    For giving and receiving love
    For taking me into battles
        and winning wars
            with your ferocious strength
    For valiantly defending your fragile tenderness
    For loving your own terrible beauty
    For revealing your deepest darkest
        to the light of discovery
            and laying open your wounds
                to the healing air
    For being willing to walk into heartbreak
        again and again
            knowing what you do
    For, even when you are shaking afraid,
        you always shout,
            "YAY!"
            "Yes"
            "Let's dance"
            &
    "I gotta have more cowbell"

Thank you for your life-giving work
Your refusal to quit
Your belief in the way I live
I adore you
I honor you
I cherish and bless your amazing work
    in my chest
        in my world
            in my relationships
                in my wanderings
I give you the gift of the best me
    in every moment we have together,
        in the brightest shining light
            I can be
We do good work, girl
    you got the beat
        oh, skip it, let's roll!

                        Yours forever true

                        P.S. I really love you

A LOVE LETTER

Wild Poems

I want to write wild poems

I want to talk of passion and death
      tell you of the short time we have here
      the important things we must do together
      how to let go of the unimportant stuff
      how to be patient and kind
      how to get intimate and be honest

I want to write naked, vulnerable words
      words that undress you and me

I want to pull you deeply into me

I want to show you my flaming desire
      feel yours burning from your side of the world
      before it's too late

I want to run and feel and sing
      and tell a thousand stories

I want to be all here
      to be real
      to see you
      to be seen
      to live through my senses
      to love with my touch

There's nothing else that is more valuable
      there's nothing else I want
      there's nothing else

Love is our Name

Share a Toast

Lost the line of development and decency.

I will wake you up just when you go to sleep good and proper to tell you a bedtime story; to remind you joy is everywhere.

There's a bit of scandal among the bohemian wildflowers, whispers concerning my impending number, advanced imperfections looming ahead.

Speaking of cool, calm, and collected...

I laugh with delicious delight at wondrous traditions, such as chocolate cake and making wishes.

I love life with all its messy, gory glory.

Love is our name.

We are the soul of the soul of the world around us, yet let none of us believe we have the power to change another;
    only the responsibility to inspire each other,
        to be our very best selves,
            to recognize beauty as beauty.

Share your favorite toast with me:

To friends and foes, and each one I'll never know- I honor you with the courage to live out loud; may we all find ourselves more than we ever expected.

Hear! Hear!

WORDS

    Words gathering like piles of leaves
    raked into a bag held wide
    Swirling, gestating
    Softly, slowly
    Sweetly, Slipping,
    Dipping, dripping
      out a small hole in the bottom
heart to hand
to pen
to paper
    At times we get clogged
      by too much, too many
We try to push,
it rarely works…

    Yet we continue
    to work
      to pursue

We sit in silence

We finally release
what needs to be written
and move into
    life afresh

Feeling much like the morning
after heavy night storms
which leaves the trees bare for winter
    The body
        The blood
            The spirit
                The soul
                    The mind
                        Must let go
                            Must purge
                                Must rest
                                    Must make way
                                        Must allow
                                    for each season's end and return
                                    for each new day to be the best it can be
                                      for each new word to be written
                                        for each new song to be sung

Legacy

Brimstone can hit the fan…

A few shocking catchphrases
create a fan base of a particular kind
Smoking guns
Chemical burns
Torches
Witch hunts
How rude do you want to be to attract that following?

It's an angry world we live upon
We are a part of that great anger, you and I
Taking delight in spewed venom
Of love
Loss
Sweet
Bitter
Who do you want to be when the smoke clears?

There is a simple truth, unvarnished
Our world is dying for lack of beauty
Salt
Light
Wisdom
Peace
The greatest leaders are not usually the loudest
What's the greatest message within us
Our passionate love story… the good news
The broken, aching world is longing for?

Healing
Grace
Mercy
Redemption
What is that something different we have to offer?

Truth is not an argument to be won
Will we make a stand on that bridge?
March, go to prison, die for the word
Gentle
Peace
Strong
Justice
Hate cannot drive out hate…

Only love will mend us, make us gentle, bring us home

In the end, what will last forever?
There is no end to God, to love, to life
To beauty
Truth
The word Kindness
Hope
Energy
Soul
What will be your epitaph,
your baton of faith to pass forward,
your legacy to leave behind?

LEGACY

The Promise

wearing pain so close to the skin
brutally displayed on arms, legs and necks
topical grief, as yet unprocessed
waiting patiently to be subsumed
within a shattered heart
carrying an unknown feeling
can be so hard to understand
tears drown our morning
watering flowered pillowcases each night
tides carrying us here and there
life blooms upside down
inside out
torn from headlines
of familial disasters

wait in hope, my friend
all is not lost
the windmills of the gods are grinding away
ever so slowly
yet the hourglass will never stop running
the fine sands of Father Time continue
the winds will change direction
you will smile again
and live to share your truest love another day
the promise is always
Yes and *Amen*
the sun is just beginning to shine through the clouds
we will run, laugh and jump in puddles
together
before this day is through

Time to Celebrate

Carrying heavy things
      into the past
      just so I can
      lay them down on a convenient corner
      and continue on around the bend
      without the load I've borne beforehand
The next light years ahead
      will be easy like Sunday morning
Songs and friends of yesterday
      returning to play new verses
      versions of ourselves yet to be
      coming to the forefront
Stages set with beauty
Bells ringing all around the glorious trees
      and rooftops

What's the next best step?

When's the celebration?

Pop the cork, baby
Let's start today
Look at what you've accomplished
      in such a short span of life
Count the days a complete success
There is no such thing as failure, anyway
Look me in the eye and give me your best defense
Then, look forward into the shining future
      and tell me how much you love me

Let peace descend onto the earth
Let it begin
      again and again
      with me

Speak

Let the world go
to rest awhile,
then be still in this nothingness
of a world awaiting birth
until you can let what wants to come
find you.

In this morning's tender light
and delicate shadows,
release all your dreams
which died unexpectedly last night.

Sit awhile with this momentary glimpse of eternity,
found within your paralyzing grief,
this surprising grand canyon of void within.

Feel small within your new vast emptiness,
watch it slowly spreading out in front of you to the north.

Awaken to this reverberating call for you
to allow your rising
to be like the hawk floating free
in the bluest skies you've ever seen.

Only when you are ready:
get up,
make your bed,
open the unlocked door,
then open your whole self to speak
those holy words you have found
carved into your gravestone;
those words which the fire has refined
into purest gold;

the words that define your life,
true and beautiful.

These words
will be recognized only by your soul;
no one else will know them;
you alone will know for sure.

These are the words
you will use to create a new heaven
and a new earth,
where the lion and the lamb will walk as best friends.

Speak with the authority you have earned
by letting everything
that did not belong to you
go its own way
with your highest blessing.

Your speaking now
will draw back the deep blue velvet curtain
of the darkest night,
revealing that great star pointing toward Bethlehem,
exploding in wild joy,
and the angels still singing stanzas of
    "Glory to God in the highest"
at your amazing, graceful arrival
home,
at last,
into the glorious music of your own
unwavering,
stable,
passionate
heartbeat.

THIS MOMENTARY GLIMPSE
OF ETERNITY

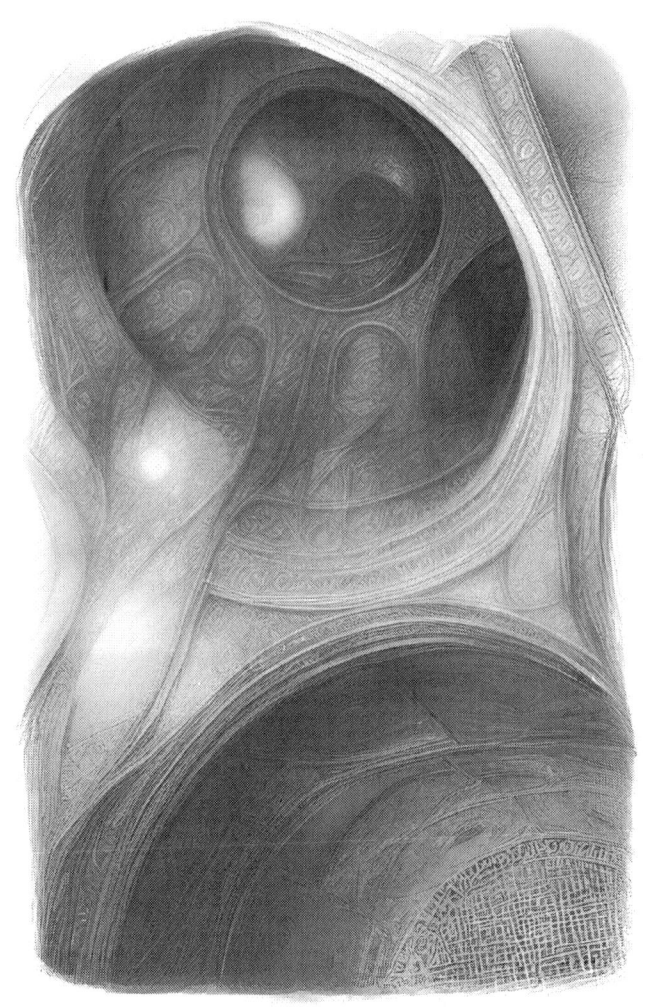

FOUR MILES

After the four miles had come and gone
and the three tenors had paused abruptly
my two legs stopped to design some landscapes
plant a few hedged borders
build a moat
or maybe several

the forsythia's flame had burned to the ground in minutes
I had no cake
so I sat eating a protein bar by the ocean
(literally, though the sensual strength of it makes me smile)
sand, definitely, all up in my business
I lay, watching the blue-and-white swirls
birds up high, teaching me to trust
the sun making a last stand atop the tree-lined water…
well, what more do I need to say…

breathing deep
achieving serenity
smelling favorites
the erotic mixture of charcoal and meat
mixed with freshly-mown grass
I floated in tune with the laughter of children
fading in and out as they ran until breathless

there was nothing sexy
about the couple loudly talking of staff meetings
beside the water's edge
but the feather left on the path in front of me
on my way home
spoke of wisdom meant just for me
I carried it home in my pocket

I used to miss you on a Friday night
now I make an important discovery
as I slowly make my way home
between sitting on freshly-cut stumps
and old stone bridges
writing poems on the path
now I'm much too busy to miss you
being at peace
with my own lyrics
being in love
with my own life

Circles

I create my first circle at 4:37am
    standing in the silence
    shadows and light reflected
    allowing the deepest internal work
    of unknowing to gestate
    seeds, yet to crack,
    words, yet to come
    deep calling to deep
    the greatest spiritual mystery
    there is no explanation for when, or how,
    the Pheonix rises triumphant
    after waiting in the cold dark
    for so long, seemingly dead
    not yet ready
    or knowing how to bloom
    into the colors of new dreams
    with roots spreading as maps
    across the pages of unwritten futures
I am letting go of all my clinging
    dead flowers thrown away
I am opening a fresh book of paper
    erasing the old black ink staining my fingers
    no longer needing to cling to what didn't work
    ready to be reminded
    this is a new day full of beauty
Creation is ever changing to meet me
    in this very moment
    everything is coming into balance
I am satisfied with what is
    right in this moment
I am eager for more than I could ever imagine
    in the ones upcoming
The sun is faithfully coming up
    as I return to my bed to sleep

Letting Go

Letting go into the wind
        the winding road behind obliterated

Creating a heart of sand inside
        then allowing the salt water to wash it clean

Ready for new footprints
        of children ready to play

Creating circles of care

Evolution of spring into summer brings so much new
        green growth, flowers

Honey bees can't resist pollination

Making love brings birthdays galore
        one after another

Blessing heaped on blessing
        grace upon grace
        mercies for this day

We wear our sunshine if needed

We sing praises until we're done
        then walk on down to the river
        feeling emotional

Baptism is one of the simplest pictures
        of a brand-new life

Colors of Pain

who knew my pain would have such brilliant colors?

such intense shades of red, yellow, green
      flaming neon orange
      the most shocking pink you can imagine
no bland grey pain will do for me
      no dark night will hold me captive
I light up the sky and shake the earth's foundations
      with my despair
      with the very abundance of my 'why me?'s
I will take all the oxygen in the room
I will explode like a blazing star
      yet it will never be enough
When I speak the heavens tremble and planets begin to fall

I will demand to be released from the grimy, peeling,
      poorly-painted prison walls where I find myself
I will demand every damn day to get what I want
I will demand my colors be the brightest in the land
      why would they not?

I demand my genie lamp be refilled with endless wishes
      it's only fitting

I say,
>   *I will walk in the light*
>   *no matter the cost*

I will spark fire in the dark
    no matter if it causes forest fires
    no matter who dies of fright
I will conquer the night with my one endless question
    repeated over and over and over
I will paint myself as myself, as a reflection of what I want
I will fight and fight and *fight*
I will not go down with the ship
I simply *will not* understand
I simply *will not* surrender
I simply *will not* continue to suffer
I will continue to paint the world
    with all the vibrant colors
    of my intensely shaded, publicized pain
that is what I *will* do

who knew my pain would be so colorful?

I'm pretty amazed at that shocking blue
    I just conjured up with my anger
that razzle-dazzle raspberry
    I just made pop with my angst

COLORS OF PAIN

I WILL WALK IN THE LIGHT
NO MATTER THE COST

ORDINARY

I wake up with 606 miles to go
I remember to remember
this day is my gift
let me not forget to wonder in the ordinary
to see beyond my own tired eyes
gazing into the language of mountains,
valleys, trees and hawks
let me not forget the beauty behind me
this time with friends and family
these celebrations of blessed union
this music, the love of my heart
let me be grateful and light-hearted
for the beauty yet to be
this time with my children and making new friends
this place to carve into home
the music playing always
ready to walk into the room with me

yes, this is an ordinary day
I will drive so many miles
I will be exhausted and ready to land
well before the end
but, really, this is no ordinary day…

there is no such thing
every day is a wonderland
full to the top with gifts of goodness
let me see each of them
let me scribe them into my soul
let me bow and say thank you
let me share them with another
let me wake tomorrow to find another ordinary,
not-so-ordinary day

Run to the Sea

Run to the sea
Say, *I flow*
      over and over
Until you are swept away
By your own water

Stand on solid ground
Say, *I surrender*
      over and over
Until you feel the thread
Binding you to the center of everything

Sit in the wind
Say, *I believe*
      over and over
Until you soar above the clouds
And fly with the angels into worlds
      you have never seen before

Swim with the whales
Say, *I am*
      over and over
Until you know their songs by heart
And they lead you into the starry sky
      on the path only they know

Fall into the silence
Say nothing
      over and over
Until you hear the voice
Which only silence can speak

Define Happiness

What makes your definition of happiness?
How do you love to disappear?
Forget your discomfort in who you are?
How your skin doesn't quite fit at times?
How you sometimes forget to button your collar?

What makes your life complete?
Do you know, beyond doubt, that you are beloved?
Forget your need to be selfish?
Your purpose found naturally
Beyond the quotes and spiritual dogma
       held with your bones?
Beyond the desire to pontificate on your held knowledge
       and superior wisdom?

What makes you feel ecstasy?
How do let go into the mystery?
Forget the world exists beyond this very moment?
Becoming one with the whales and the sea
Singing songs you had forgotten in this lifetime?
Swimming into the place where sea and sky
       seamlessly connect?

What makes you dance, sway, move with grace?
What makes you sing at the top of your lungs,
    belt the wrong lyrics,
      find the harmony part?
Forget you're not alone in the car, the office, the world?
Allowing who you are to shine?
Allowing who you are to be enough?
Allowing who you are to be everything you need to be?

It's Not Easy

it's not easy
to do the hard thing
to lose
to stand
to eat
to sleep alone
to wait at all
much less
to be long-time patient
to be strong
to allow the pain
to allow the grief
the tears of exhaustion
frustration
weariness
to press on
to refuse to settle
to believe, in spite of loss
to sing on the shores of exile
to fight in the face of minority
to keep the warm fire
to build wells in dry places
to send out love
to melt our defenses
to keep touching the lepers
to allow healing to come
to ruthlessly keep letting go
to rise above our stories
to inhabit them completely
to set our boundaries
yet keep our hearts open
to be prepared
to live ready
to keep saying *yes*

Momma Said It

There will be days
    of no words
        no space
            no breath
                no time
                    no priority
Days I will lose
    in the fog of life
Spans of time I will walk through
    without finding much gentle
    or recognizing beauty
Times when my world spins sideways
    my head dizzy
    my body nauseated by the air I breathe
There will be days
    when hands fall heavy
    and feet feel like they are encased in cement
There will be days of endless crying
    of staying in bed
    of sneezing a million times
        (At least it feels that way)
    of watery eyes and brutal headaches
There will be days of stress
    of overwhelm
        of unanswered questions
        of Why? *Oh, Why?*
            of grief
                of grime
                    of grim
                        of gritty

Yes, there will be days like this

Yes, Momma said it
    and she's nearly always right…

But!

Even with those hard days
    they will not be everyday
    they will not last

To every turn
    there is a return
To every circle
    an encircling
To everything
    there is a season
To every loss
    there is a gain
To every morning
    there is a mercy
To every night
    there is a light waiting
To every single moment
    there is a blessing and a grace

Psalms

I cannot walk in the world
   with shaded eyes
      tho wishes lie bruised on cold marble floors
         waiting for a death blow
            as only they can know death
               a wheel within a wheel
I will walk through the garden path
   even through winter
      rejoicing that spring will come
I will walk in all kinds of weather
   and sit in the sand or on the rain-soaked bench
      feeling aliveness creep into my chilly bones
         as I flirt with the seagulls
            and wise old magnolia trees
I will walk the circling path again and again
   wedded to joy at the hearts strewn along
      my every spiraling pathway
I will cross and recross the bridges
   I do not choose to burn
      bridges built strong and sturdy
         waiting to carry me over
            into the next place
I will have my cakes and ale
   and eat and drink yours, too
      then lie down
         surrounded by peace
            in cool blue pastures
               along with my favorite Psalms
                  and a bit o' William Shakespeare

Poetry in an Hour or So

and so it begins…

the heart gathering courage
arranging space
creating openings
defining time
to pour out its words
sometimes we need a bit of preparation
(sometimes we need a lot)
as we step into the flow
of giving and receiving
of these great, marvelous gifts
carving out our place in the world
as we are called to carve
finding the hidden figures
within the rock of our hearts
beauty sculpted in honest measure
time within time
moments frozen
on Trees sacrificed in our memorials
oh, that we may write these testaments
hearts burned to ashes
touched by the vulnerability
of our naked resurrection
hands of raw emotion
drenched in ink
made of our own blood
each drop measured in grace
revealed through the work of our words
love of our lives
wrestled
written
spoken
lived

WHAT MATTERS?

Wisdom doesn't always go bone marrow-deep
Maybe the best we can hope for
is not to be consistently foolish

Maybe the only risk we should keep attempting
is the one where the only loss
is that the bookie gets the VIG

What if everything else has no possibility
to get us anywhere?

What if magic doesn't actually exist?
What if vanity is vanity, all is vanity?

What if the ground
just won't bear our weight anymore?

What if we never get to see it happen?

What if love skips my generation?
What if it's true, I'm just not lovable?
What if I really am too much of a good/bad thing?
What if you and I
are not capable of trusting ever again?

What if I never make it home?

What if there are never any good choices
or solid ground?

What if love is too much of a burden
for us mortals to bear?
Too much of a cost to consider?
Too much of an unnatural commodity
in this current landscape
of our tinseltown world?

What if there is no comfort or joy?
What if heaven is an illusion
and life is nothing more than pain?
Is life still worth living?
Is there still goodness to be had?
Something still to fight for?

What if God just doesn't care that much
about the suffering we experience?

What if this is the last heart-based risk I ever take?
What matters then?

WHAT MATTERS?

Yesterday

yesterday I was born a leaf
a small fragile tender wisp
trembling as I hung on the vine

yesterday I hung as mist above the marshgrasses
softly whispering to the birds soaring above me
as they taught me to sing songs of freedom
into each new morning

yesterday I was a gust of air
short-lived, but not insignificant
full of bone-rattling cold
and hot disturbing bravado

yesterday I was a large, slow, snowflake
plopping down like a wet goose feather
making the world a magical place

yesterday I was a world made of glass
lying shattered on the floor
hoping to be recycled into a new and useful planet

yesterday I was various people-
a student, a host, a friend, a lover
feeling my way into the next moment
hoping to find a way home

yesterday I was a tall tree
proud yet with humble confidence
accepting the grief that winter brings
gently weeping
waiting for spring

yesterday I was a large, dependable mountain
made of sheer delights to behold and explore
all along the way
the greens of my valleys
the grandeur of my peaks
leaving me breathless and in awe
at every step of my life's grand adventure

YESTERDAY
I WAS A TALL TREE

So Completely

What if
    by practicing presence
        so completely
I have forgotten
    the past
    the future
    all eternity
        and I have also forgotten
            my desire
            my dreams
            my hopes?

What if
    by practicing patience
        so completely
I have forgotten
    to take action
    my momentum
    personal goal-setting
        and I have also forgotten
            to laugh to play
            my creativity and my spontaneity?

What if,
    by practicing surrender
        so completely
I have forgotten
    to set boundaries
    to apply self-care
    to find stability
        and I have also forgotten
            personal preferences
            to love luxury
            to create my personal lifestyle?

What if,
    by practicing non-attachment
        so completely
I have forgotten
    to take ownership
    to stand responsibly
    the definition of commitment
        and I have also forgotten
            to feel joy
            to move with freedom
            to remember the worth of you and me?

What if,
    by becoming spiritual
        so completely
I have forgotten
    to have balance
    to embrace being human
    to give gratitude and live humbly
        and I have also forgotten
            to show kindness
            to share compassion
            to feel every possible feeling?

What if
    I have everything "right"
    I have achieved "enlightenment"
    I have practiced perfection
    I have let go and slogged through
    I have sacrificed and sanctified
        but I have forgotten love?

What then?

Oh my God, *what then?*

SO COMPLETELY

The Vow

The day all my stories disappeared, along with everyone and everything I had ever loved, I saved myself the only way I knew how:

I stood, a sparrow in the eye of that hurricane, vowing to never take the easy way out, to never make a choice only for comfort or money, but for love- but for love alone *(though I had no clue what love truly looked like).*

Not knowing what that meant, not knowing where that path would take me, that day I walked out the first doorway into that strange world. *(I could not know, or, suffice it to say, I could not have done it if I had.)*

That day the gods cracked open my box's top and laughed heartily at my naïveté *(as they did at Pandora once upon a time).*

That day I was startled at my own powerful beauty and felt fear of the truth of myself, realizing it could destroy me if I didn't learn how to know it in its shadowy depths. *(For years I didn't recognize myself in any mirror.)* What with that branding in my forehead and the complete devastation of my inner world's landscape, I was completely disfigured, a Picasso painting of blues and blacks, imploded by the explosion I had somehow survived.

That day I also lost the songs of my motherland, those most important to me. And my voice- my voice vanished with my banishment.

I had no ability to hide from that stark moment, from that brutal and terrible truth; all my foundations and structures were gone. *(I tried to find them; gone forever.)*

So, I faced forward, toward the only light I could see *(that shadow, far away)* and I began to walk with my stranger-self, always remembering my vows, *(though made by an innocent child before she know what evils existed).* Those vows were the best of me and so I clung to them, no matter how difficult. *(I knew they were my only salvation.)*

I walked on and on, learning my own true voice, becoming a player in new stories, finding new songs which spoke to me of me. *(Blue songs of broken hearts, of longing for love, for home.)* And as I walked uphill and down into hell itself, I met strangers beside me *(beautiful angels sent to help and guide and protect me).*

Somehow, I kept the faith, alive and green and growing. *(It was given to me to carry.)*

Somehow, I kept my vows and earned a new name.

Somehow, because of those vows, I kept my hands open and my palms up *(to receive, to give, to be thankful, to bless, to be blessed).*

Somehow, I kept walking, crawling, limping through the years of death, storm, fire, poverty, falling, ever walking toward that shadow of light, toward the innocent hope that I would find love, that I would find *home.*

That I would find myself whole, and happy, and loved, and in love with my life.

And so now, after these long years of exile, I come at last to the second door with the light shining softly on the welcome sign, which bids me…*Come In.*

Holding the Secrets

holding the secrets in silence
all these cramped years of painful habits
screaming within the internal chambers
of backs and necks and shoulders

Mona Lisa vaguely smiling
echoes of wounds inflicted long ago
clinging tightly to every cell wall
reverberations within the halls of ancestral DNA

cloud walking with the storms of terror
silver linings long stripped of value
snapshots of abuse caught and carried

all these years of walking pilgrim
feet blistered and road-weary
I begin draining the swamps of false imprisonment
layer by layer

what have I so torturously considered mine-
and deservedly so?

why have I held so tightly
to the belief that self-flagellation
is my only deserved birthright?

when did I decide to build memorials of abuse
and carry them as dragging pain-filled weights
toxic marrow in my bones?

when did this pain become the outline of my identity
the blueprint of my choices?
will I let it go now that I've seen it?
will I behead this beast and allow the blood to spill?

will I allow this pain to dissolve
into a distant misty memory
of someone I used to be?
will I claim a new inheritance
of pain-free trust and love?

will I stand within the circle of my own dreams
drawn by my truest, strongest and highest self
and sing hallelujahs to the sky?

will I tap into my own unique beauty
and recognize my body's
and my life's extreme value?

will I speak the true truth
of the way my life will be
and then create it as reality?

will I bring rest to myself
each day I am blessed to live?

will I build all of these questions into new habits?

yes, I will
yes, and amen

HOLDING THE SECRETS

The Gift

My life is not tied up
in pretty blue bows.

Not many straight lines appear
on my map to this place
where I find myself today.

I've chosen to go off-grid.
Well, maybe the truth is
I *found* myself off-grid,
and after a while I realized it was the gift!
So I began making difficult-but-purpose-filled choices,
again and again,
to stay there.

I've skated thin ice and jumped with no net
over and over, despite my own stable-craving nature.
These tough years taught me so much
in solitary silence.
I've learned that somehow
the ground always holds my weight.
The universe conspires to help me.

And so, I live mostly on the edges,
where adventure steals
all the comforts of an easy-chair existence;
where there is no sinking
into the clouded cover of "safety";
when risking it all
in the danger zone
of unconditional loving
takes everything you have.
A complex living
of big picture purpose;
of loving the world enough
to sacrifice pride
to stay small and humble.

Does anything I do matter?
Sometimes I'm not sure.
But if anything does,
then everything does!

And so it goes,
and so it goes...

THE GIFT

ONE

in the world between worlds
where the shimmering abstract
holds all the secrets within us
words are absent
no scripture exists
there are no definitions
as there is no need for such things
in our eternal knowing
we are ever being known
the mystic colors of God fill us
unseeable in this earthly realm's obscured vision
they hold us there
where we don't need to be understood
or understand anything
we are simply
all we could ever hope to be
we are the lover and the beloved
eternal love
eternally loved
complete
You and I
I in You
one

MAYBE

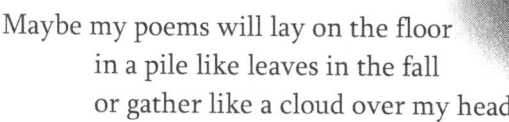

Maybe my poems will lay on the floor
    in a pile like leaves in the fall
    or gather like a cloud over my head

Maybe my words will rain from my pen
    like a summer thunderstorm
    quick and lightning-sharp
    tearing souls asunder

Maybe all the books of poetry I will ever write
    will rise like a flock of birds
    and fly south for the winter

Maybe I'll find just the right words
    needed to paint a perfect sunset
    but until then I'll stand in simple wonder
    with dazzled eyes

Maybe the dance of the cobra
    will arise from my hips
    every time I listen to the high tide at night
    or the sound of your laughter

Maybe the most beautiful love songs
    will drip from my mouth in waves
    drowning the pain of your broken heart

Maybe one day I will speak
    with the tongues of men and angels
    while having love
    and watch the world change forever

I Am the Fire

I am the fire on the mountain
I am the fire by the sea
I am the fire in the forest
Burning down the trees

I am the fire in the desert
I am the fire in the snow
I am the fire that will warm you
When your bones have grown cold

I am the fire for your shelter
I am the fire for your bread
I am the fire for your hunger
Whenever you go to bed

I am the fire on the water
I am the fire that is near
I am the fire burning your words
Consuming your doubt and your fear

I am the fire of your longing
I am the fire of your soul
I am the fire of your loving
I will never grow cold

I am the fire for your winter
I am the fire for your spring
I am the fire of your living
Passion I will bring

I am the fire of destruction
I am the fire where you die
I am the fire of your Pheonix
As you rise, as you soar, to the sky

AWARE

I've seen the sun shine like diamonds
On a thousand different waters
I've seen buttercups bloom in winter
And so many primroses
Bloom along the garden path
I've seen willows stand beside me, dry-eyed
While I could not contain myself
And still waters overflowed
I've been stalked by hawks and hounds
Found hearts of every size and sort
Along the garden path
I've seen the world turn upside down
I've seen the ring of fire
I've met the King of Everything
I've fought my own desire
And now my steps are turning home
My heart is full
My feet quite sore
My roots are sinking in the ground
My name is on the door
There's beauty all around me
And I'm very well aware
That life is now beginning
With all I've waited for

WILLOWS STAND BESIDE ME,
DRY-EYED
AS STILL WATERS OVERFLOW

MEANWHILE

Meanwhile, back at the resurrection,
night has turned to day.
Here I stand amazed
at my own rebirth,
dazed and a bit confused,
eyes blinking in the morning sun,
attempting to adjust.
I am completely changed
from my life-to-death-back-to-life experience,
more than a bit claustrophobic
(due to the burial, no doubt).

I am no longer sure
if my bank account is active
or my passport is still relevant.
How will I go on from here in the world now?
What will my friends and family do
with this who-is-now me
*(they are done with grief
and moved along with life in-between)?*

I am, for sure, no longer the way I used to be.
I have, for sure, experienced things
they will never understand;
I have flown with angels
and seen what lies beyond the Milky Way.
I have, for sure, left my fear behind me
in that fresh, unmarked grave.
I know, for sure, there will be no turning back,
no compromise of this wild and exquisite thing
beating within me,
this life of mine is mine
(this heartbeat's miracle will be a never-forgotten gift).

I can only take this first step
away from this boneyard,
named and dated with final markers;
a place I no longer belong.
I can only start close in,
in silent reverie walking
along this uncharted path,
which will only be revealed by my footsteps.
I discard my grave clothes
and turn to see the colors of my new self shining.
I take a small shaky step
and find the ground holds my weight
(breathe deep-
inhale, exhale).

Soon I will attempt to speak
with my new voice.
There is a song being written
(which must be sung);
a beauty seeking to burst
(which will no longer be denied);
a love now known
(which can never be unknown).

I raise my hands and kiss the sky;
I bow my knees and kiss the ground.
I rise and begin the journey
through the next narrow gate
mysteriously painted
with the wondrous word:
LIFE

Everybody's Writing a Book

Everybody's writing a book
      full to the edges
      with stories of brokenness
      smutty sensational stuff
      sex, drugs
      rock and roll and handguns
      prison time
      and scandals with the local preacher
I'm too tired to tango
      coming to terms with my own past
At least at the present moment
      I am resting in the knowledge
      that I am just enough
      though not that special after all
      which makes me laugh out loud
I no longer carry the world on my shoulders
      Atlas has long ago faded from the scene
I'm holding up my piece of the blue sky
      and it requires my full attention
I rest in any spare moment I can garner
      ever learning this afresh:
          God equals love!
Triangle becomes circle
      as does every other shape of the heart
I smile a little as I step onto this sparkly stage
      gloriously lighted
      by personal security
I simply open my mouth
      and sing

I Like the Idea

I like the idea
   of absorption
      disappearance
         melting into
            life
               as I know it

Getting lighter
   after the stormy midnight
      or fall back morning

Fog fading
   into mountains
      trees
         rivers
            bridges rising out of mist

Hardening into the shape
   of integrity
      holding open
         the way between us
            standing security
               of life as we know it
                  and the good life to come

Nature shows us the way
   always
      to live beautifully
         to let go easily
            to bloom naturally
               to move in right time
                  and in season
                     to settle into grace
                      to pour out love

Wonder

every morning I wake up with wonder
at where I am
at what is happening
in this moment
how phat my days are
how rich this morning's avocado on toast
how abundant this morning sunshine
how freely the windmills turn
how beds of gold and grey
hold me so very tenderly in the night
how moments we enter into with another
can brings such unlimited expansion
how a tender act can change the chemistry
of the whole world
how four dollars can change someone's whole day
how much there is beyond ourselves
and every sip is as sweet as the nectar of the gods
of how we get to do it
we get to choose it
every moment
of every day
as a prayer
as a song
as a gift

WARRIOR

I bump into myself from a place in time:
>I remember how the sun arose
>and how the light turned into a myriad
>of brilliant chips of jewels,
>rocks of gold and silver
>sparkling in this garden of grace;
>kaleidoscope of beauty,
>winter roses blooming under blue canopies.

Sometimes things go wrong
>for year after year,
>yet the sun still brings each new day,
>full of everything.

Tomorrow is always arriving,
>ready to bring in new velvet-textured dreams;
>ready for prayers;
>for the stirring of oatmeal;
>for dirty china in the sink.

I remember the way the phoenix keeps rising,
>reborn over and over
>into this current age of Aquarius.

Birth of many griefs;
>birth of ever more joys.

Birth of surrender;
>birth of courage.

Birth of hope;
>birth of presence.

Birth of many colors
>painted across the night skies,
>green vines intertwined
>through a healing, compassed heart.

Warrior:
>forever opening
>to love.

I Rise

I have taken back my own listening
      as I hear a battle cry.
      Awaken, dear heart,
      come back home-
           Fight on!

The weeping cherries have cried their last for me this spring.
      They are spent and ragged from their bouts
      with this wracking grief.
      Their puddles of pink tears lie on the ground
      around their footed trunks.

We have eaten cake, you and I.
      We've shared a toast or two,
      full of promises and new love.

The dogwoods and lilacs having patiently waited
      and now bloom just for me.
      Perfumed air follows me
      for all these miles and miles.

My heart is still,
      paused,
      spell-bound.

I am full and empty at the same time.
      Life is always bitter,
      always sweet,
      always both at once.

Flaming bushes hatch their eggs
      and throw holy joy into the blue sky.
      My tears find their way to the ocean,
      mingling with their many brothers and sisters.

Freedom is never free.
> The cost is always found on the edge
> of a cruel man's sword.
> Jesus is always lead away to be crucified.

I lay on feathers of lost innocence,
> those birds plucked for my dinner.
>> I will eat with relish.

My body, adjusting to this new age,
> bleeds and burns;
> bleeding out, burning away
> those old days,
> all my dreams,
> poured out red,
> gone up in smoke.

This present moment must be all I need to trust.

I wonder what will become of me in these nexts:
> in these next new beginnings,
> in the unknown upcomings,
> in these wild wonders,
> in these deep blue yonders.

I breathe again.
I stay in the fight.
I open my heart again.
I feel alive again.

I cry.
> I pray.
>> I sleep.
>>> I rise.
>>>> I rise.
>>>>> *I rise.*

I RISE

THROW HOLY JOY
INTO THE BLUE SKY

Follow the Light

I decline all offers to live in a house of reasons and proofs.
I refuse to live a moment without the faith of doubt.
I reject staying in the box of absolute truths.
I deny my own dogged dogma
        of black-and-white knowledge.
I challenge myself continually to keep letting go
        of what I know for sure.
I intentionally say *no*
        to my own sense of pride and privilege.
I humbly confess my own lack of humble speech.
I gratefully open myself to the vast newness of each day
I necessarily choose to rely on God
        rather than myself.
I stand on the foundational stone
        of believing life is always for me
                even when I can't see it.
I embrace change, understanding its value,
        even when it's a struggle
                and it feels difficult for me.
I bow on the shores of the ocean of goodness and pain
        as I find my place
                among all the grains of sand.

I sit in the most comfy seat of miraculous realization:
    I am a drop in the ocean;
        I am the ocean in a drop.
I stand on the circle of the earth and speak
    to the wind and the fire,
        to the stars and the dirt.
I am water- I flow;
I am earth- I grow.
I am that I am that I am that I am.
Abundance in every breath:
    ashes to ashes,
        dust to dust.
I rise,
    I fall.
I live,
    I die.
I love;
    I love.
I follow the light-
    I follow the light.

A Love Letter to the Light

I am so honored and grateful to be part of the birth and delivery of this book of poetry. Over the years, my dear friend Amy has followed her own bright light, bringing forth these tender, eccentric, love-filled pages of poetry. Even as she has known the depths of darkness, still she relentlessly seeks and taps into her own light, boldly sharing it with us now.

Isn't it crazy how paths collide, how our lives evolve just like a poem or a song?

For Amy and I, it all started in a booth filled with vintage Words + Art. The air was crisp early-autumn cool, her smile and eyes, gentle all-season warm.

We both felt it, standing there small-talking. Yes, we knew straight away we were on the verge of a living poem in progress - kindred spirits, soul sister, *anam kara* - bumping into an ancient contract, epic and old, yet oh so sweet and new.

I first learned about Amy's poetic tendencies when she shared her newsletter, *Songs from the Valley*, chock full of the sensual art, music and poetry she collects everywhere she goes. In these publications, she shone the light on so many poets, writers and musicians, skillfully weaving new tapestries again and again. To this day, I am awed by her dedication to this ongoing compilation and encourage those who are new to her work to check them out.

Through the years, we have step-by-stepped through our own labyrinthine lives, sharing countless words and conversations, surrendering to bouts of laughter, walking one another through times of grief and tears. Beyond our personal friendship for nearly a decade, we joined forces to co-create sacred retreats, inviting other women to collaborate and find their own poetic voices.

Amy has a very special capacity to stand in her strength and power, while extending grace and deep truth. For years, we have shared poetry - our own and others - with such natural, easy love and respect. As a writer who often belabors over the editing process, the structure, format and worthiness of my words on a page, I have admired the way Amy invites and allows her words to flow, trusting that they show up just as they are meant to be. Amy also constantly reads and studies poetry and poets, seeing the whole world through a poet's eyes as she discovers the beauty.

This book of poetry is a gift of light and love. I invite you, as you read these poems, to delve into each one, searching for the lessons, inspiration, light and love they offer you.

Robin Christine O'Neal

Acknowledgments

I would like to thank my readers,
especially
Robin Christine O'Neal
& Charles Cooper.

I want to thank Debrah Englert,
my fabulous hair wizard,
& also
my daughter Krista
for editing and photo curating,
& my son Brandon,
illustrator extraordinaire!

And finally, a huge thank you goes out to Ray,
for loving me & helping me achieve my dreams.

About the Author

Amy Duvall-Mehringer is a singer, poet, writer, and inspirational speaker currently residing in North Carolina.

From 2008 to 2013, Amy published an art-driven, bi-monthly newsletter named *Songs of the Valley*. From 2011 to 2021, she maintained a daily poetry/art blog called Life: Acoustic and Amplified.

In Follow the Light, Amy seeks to share her journey of hope along the path of healing and encourage others to move forward as she did.

Amy's new music CD, #Love Letters on the Path, is now available by email request!

Website: amyduvall.com
Email: amyduvallmusic.com

Hold on!
Never quit!
We can do hard things!
Life is good!

No matter how difficult
life becomes,
the tide will turn
and life will be sweet again.

Made in the USA
Columbia, SC
13 November 2023